#irl

Poems

by

Matthew
David
Wachsman

Visit online at matthewdavidwachsman.com

Cover Design by Matthew David Wachsman
Text set in Baskerville
Subjects: Poetry | Family & Relationships - Life Stages | Political
Science - Political Ideologies

Paperback ISBN: 979-8-9868685-0-9
Hardcover ISBN: 979-8-9868685-1-6
E-ISBN: 979-8-9868685-2-3

To my father and weekend poet, David S. Wachsman, who made with blood and love, a way to add these words to the world. I will never know whether they are worthy of so great a man, but they are all my blood and love could make.

Words, words and more words
These tiny black ink lifeboats
Float on paper ponds

Empathy without awareness is indifference.

#irl
by Matthew David Wachsman

heart started
tick
I cry on emerging from womb
and begin a finite life
strolling through unused hours
across todays focused on tomorrows
days when nothing happens
months that don't matter
and years of coasting
my impermanence
shrugged off
each footfall nearer an end
I may never
know how to believe
but now I want
to win
need
to light up every feeling
and burn them hot as sun
my life consuming me
leaving no smoke
nor ash
gasping all the air
into and out
from lungs and flesh
every bit of bone
and clockworks: my heart
lived all the way through
until there is
nothing left
but witness marks

We did it
A job well done
Triumphs of art hung to ceilings
(unseen)
filled with noble angels, intimate angles and vertigo hues
pieces with pulses
whose deep breath could flush your face
And music
(unheard)
penetrating
like heat
that would fuse the shattered glass of you
Books to sate and educate
(unread)
with refreshing perspectives and breakthroughs
wisdom and loves that outlast the tales
words sewing wings
to re-awaken dreams of
soaring

We can make ourselves glorious
pause the brushes, cameras, pens and keyboards
heal eyes with unviewed art
restore buoyancy to heavy hearts
through immersion in archived music
awaken resolve while on odysseys in old books
cease creating anything disposable
then look at and love
everything on earth
we did not make
Permit trees to reclaim the land
and
Give leave to animals that they be
allowed
to survive
Lives are indeed the greatest works of all
Instead we monetize clicks
#monetizeclicks #poem #museumpieces #irl
seeking payment for what we make
shelve almost all
refuse the past and accept the future
(untenable)

2

It is always the same
a quickened pulse
the arm rises
in defiance
of gravity

You relish the work the
walk across the
stage the
award the
toast and admiring
words Cherish the
realization

You made it.

Success is a summit but
temporary One
more wondrous souvenir
which fades

You were
born and survived
never again to do
anything
so appreciated

But you will keep
trying

An Era of Lightning

An infant listens to thunder
The gentle chorus
trampolining on streets, houses and hills
like a rabid band of automaton players
clap drum slap shoe smashing ground in soft blur

A mother speaks with soothing assurance
at the distance
all is well with the world, child
all is well
all one tiny instant's convergence
of hot and cold
of light and blinding darkness

Father and Son

I cry until I wake my daddy and I make the sun rise
returning things to how I want
Daddy tells me it is what the sun does
that it will always come back
as long as I wait

And then he died
and I did not cry
I waited
never thinking
he could not be sure
whether on that one day it was my waiting
or my tears
which brought him back

Pleasure

you can swallow this feeling whole
my mighty joy
rushing upstream in boisterous river
vigorous, vital and free
this rapturous body
pure me made pure you
writhing at the very height of its power
or you can hope these words
are woven net
extracting it from native waters

shall I remove its bones and brains?
Thickly coat in cheese and sweetness?

Go ahead
eat it bite-sized
or behold my feeling alive
and set free
in all its fullness
to jump and romp
on its journey
to you
your pleasure so boundless
as to swarm and overrun mind
wordless
like a smile

Irrepressible thoughts restrained
the synaptic straps
snapping
The shoulder blades pulled back like stones in sling shots
The masseter muscles pressing teeth into teeth
An uprising of syllables
massing
and rising up the well
The bucket beneath the rope
flooding over from heavy raindrops
Abdomen pressing guts into spine
wringing two saturated sponges of air
Lateral jaw muscles compress
lowering the drawbridge of the mouth
A hurricane slamming up the trachea
heaving at the straining doors just before
the larynx
she speaks

a single source
feeds many rivers
a clear water flood of words
carves paths deep and wide
greening the arid earth alive
and unleashing in us an unforgiving torrent
blast sprays, projectiles, insults and mud
fusing into a smothering blanket
of angry sludge
drowning people
polluting the sea
and the air and from there
everyone

Hey, check this out:
Pablo Picasso runs his skateboard down a guardrail
hairpin turns to a sidewalk piano
launches himself off the board
lands in a handstand
and back bends onto piano bench
a move henceforth known as "A Full Pablo"
then improvises
something so beautiful, piercing
and full of sharp keys
my heart is cut
and I melt
unlocked and opened
onto the ground

"In the style of Brahms," I whisper
"Early Dvorak," he replies
then jumps up
hits "stop" on recorder
Signs and sells the skateboard
the keyboard
and the recording
then spray paints a portrait:
"Banksy Spray Painting a Wall"
on a wall
riffing on Banksy
and better
because it is a Picasso
"You should save the world," I say
squinting
at Picasso eclipsing sun
"That's what I'm doing," he replies
"why aren't you?"
shrugs
has lunch
draws a harlequin
in marker
and signs it
for the restaurant staff
then murmurs to himself
"Where to next?"

8

My Message To You

You think you can discern good from evil
But that ability does not exist
You want to be understood
about beliefs you do not understand

You do not feel enough
No one does
Fear and love are
lost in equal measure
when the illusion of safety is worth more than affection

This is my message just for you
Focus on my words
as I whisper your name
in the space between lines

Learn more about that thing you are afraid of
(I am whispering your name)
like so many others who confronted this same fear
(I am whispering your name)
Learn until you accept you're somewhat wrong about it
(I am whispering your name)
and others were right all along
(I am whispering your name)
then you will be able to love everyone
(I am whispering your name)
your loss can become real
(I am whispering your name)
and you can begin to live
(I am whispering your name)
at last

I love you,

signed
(I am whispering your name)

We are dismissible
comprehensible
truth-wailing lighthouses
in fog
ignored
lest anyone be annoyed

We shout
warnings
for it might not be too late
only to watch involuntary confessions
in narrowing eyes
they know what's right
but prefer what's wrong
most of the rest resolved to remain lost in chokehold mist
their hulls trespassing
a wreck and rock-strewn sea

Feathery mounds of parchment skin
sag under eyes
like burlap sacks
ready to catch tears
the world is made for us now
as it ever was

Compass point lurches
as screeching light speed electrostatic bursts
fire the answer into synapses
careening past gasping blood
drunk with exertion
piercing the chaos of a frantic desperate
free-fall twisting spasmodic
all-thresholds-breached
primal final
lunge
for
a
single
heat-seared sun-blind
vision
of what matters

11

Upon this page
there is a character
just like you
or you, perhaps

Feel the lungs of Shakespeare
like yours now
slowly exhaling self-poisoned air while you consider
what words will come and what they might mean
sitting at a desk reciting
recently written lines
lit by eastern sun through yonder window
seeing like you
with eyes like Shakespeare's
and ears hearing you speak your words

"and Juliet is the sun"

words of longing and lust
like they were his
but written for another
character to live
like they are your words
Romeo's lava boiling up inside
the magma of your love cresting caldera
and smothering you
under a roof of liquid rock
agitating for a single burning breath
filling with self-poisoned air
splattering pages
turning table to ash
and inside you
the realization
you are breathless
at the very precipice of your great love
as Romeo
before Juliet
when he
loved Rosalind
needed her
wooed her
then lost her
his air breathed out

adding to clouds more clouds
with deep sighs
these words of Shakespeare's
about you
like Romeo

only after Rosalind
and midnight heartbreak
could break light like a sun's
Juliet
or would that light die
and make possible
true love after Juliet
like a fresh breath
the One
your life full of vows
unlike Romeo (self-poisoned)
or Shakespeare
his bones long unmoved
Your life
including a character
just like you
or you, perhaps
with a heart
for her
alone

Their Promise

she will lift and shake the sign she will
then drop
run into his arms
through his clothes and flesh
and hold him
shedding plural like
a curable burden

this time
they will never let go

the thought of it filled the emptiness between horizons
her sign held aloft at the heavens
then dropped
her impatient arms shattering the air
cracking the shackles
of gravity and other obligations to earth
she would trespass the vast and endless sky
to hold him in a sunbath
and they would never let go
even as light drained
and he was reduced
to the shape of his skin across her hands
the sense of his desire
and his growing relief
the sound of his breathing
filling the entire
universe
like glue
until everything stopped
perfectly

No devil met me at the dusty dirt
crossroads
just bones and sallow skin hanging inside wrinkled black suit
slid one foot forward then the other next to it
lowered fedora to shield his bad eye
pulled a ball of crumpled paper
from jacket pocket and let it roll
from a skeletal hand
his impossibly long fingernails
black with dirt
as if papers
had been retrieved from a grave
me bent over
giving the ground my attention
grabbing pen from dress pants
and squeezing young fingers around those cursed and precious pages
feeling his stare blossom
like a red flower
opening to me
as I flattened each and every page, not bothering to read and signed.

No.
I practiced.

I saw guns in movies
and yearned to pull triggers
Music in cars
made me want to perform

When I was young
and would have been up for either
three of us played army
our toy soldiers dying and killing on small hill
Then we pulled translucent plastic pistols
purple, orange and red
us scattering like shrapnel
for cover
laughing and vicious
skinny everything and carrying watery death
in tiny hands
not like we were evolving into killers
but that we were born this way
never to suffer
for the adulations of this art

My mother wished me to have music lessons
sit at the piano and play
and while I cannot say it felt as natural
the instrument was no different than
a gun
in my hands
once I got good enough to work it
and fingers could trigger notes
to fly at intended targets

My hero's hands
played
for death
and resurrection
until fingers were silenced
by the sublimation of better loves
and my decision to only bear witness to murderers and musicians

despite the depth terror can
carve its claws
skin is the only evidence
of authenticity
integrity ensuring it is
untouched by slower hands in knife fights
hesitation leaving scars
the parts that don't heal right
pointed at
to justify who we become
destiny is the jail cell one never leaves

he isn't that big
or maybe he is and I am just worked up
I'm only 11
and the knife is just a pocket knife
but I had learned the three strokes
to make him unsavable

he raises his hands
and roars a feral laugh
seeing I have not moved
he says, "I like you."
then cuts me
and I kill him
one, two, three
in my mind
my leaking blood more authentic than the story I will tell
of how it was my decision to let him go
and get help

The Art of the Fugue

JS Bach was prolific
in music and bedroom
proud of his sons
and their popular tunes

He must have known
work would be his legacy
the boys unequal to his art
their music soon lost
while his saved and was savored

He spent his life upstream to
spawn
children his greatest joy
but his second greatest gift

JS Bach was prolific
in music and bedroom
proud of his sons
and their popular tunes

He must have known
work would be his legacy
the boys unequal to his art
their music soon lost
while his saved and was savored

He spent his life upstream to
spawn
children his greatest joy
but his second greatest gift

and the catcher who lost the ball in the sun
when the finger slipped on the high note fret
after the send button was unknowingly missed for a day
because the closing door bus stop was daydreamed
the false memory of rescue letter mailed
truthfully lying
where it had been thrust in the rush to grab the glove
the guitar send the email about the letter and
worry
the only constant in this life
everything piling on
a cat unfinished undaunted and unleashed
swipes with angry claws
tearing skin

Mozart's father took him to hangings
great fun and he clamored for more
set down sonata on staves
while composing a concerto in head
gleeful upside down and backward fingers
prance and preen
on blindfold night party champagne spree
not enough money
and the two of six children who survived, wife and always music
the rope pressing but never tight
he would prove himself to
the hangman
who was deaf
and had problems of his own

A child sits at her piano
and carefully taps out scales
until she gets them right
her smile blooms
and she explodes from the bench
into mommy's happy arms
"Can I go play now?" she asks and mommy nods.

He thinks he will barely look at her when he says it
in fact he can't look at her at all
"I love you and I've never said that to anyone before."
"Really"?
"Well except my parents,
but I love you more."
He waits and waits in silence.

The driver backs up the bus
puts it in park
hops out and helps an old man
"I'm going to be late," someone yells from the back.
Passengers applaud.

What if the future wasn't ever up to us
if it was always too late to save the planet
the sun was destined to explode
and all matter slow
to a stop?

What of it?
Can this finally be the day we get right?

The child is slammed down by
a stocky baserunner and
the ball dribbles away
in front of his parents
whose banter never wavers
from love

he looks down
and lightly kicks the dirt

then with the game on the line
the baseball comes right at his glove
and everyone turns their faces
to him

with a practiced calm
the child transfers the baseball
cups it in his palm and splayed fingers
and does his best to look casual
as he pulls back his slender arm
fires the baseball
toward the first baseman's outstretched glove
and waits to see what happens
his eyes hiding
behind sunglasses

He looks down
and kicks the dirt
as he always did
when a play was over
and he wanted to be a man

Prayers

an empty and yearning young man
still unsure of his worth
presents desire
with eyebrows
and compresses her to him
like a volume knob swung loudest
his arms clasped in a ring
shaking, distorted
and rising up in her an involuntary cringe
he goes numb
icy hands hanging from mis-rotated arms
frozen in open-handed dua
his supplication
newly denied
the path vanished and unknowable

There is a finality to now
an irreversible push away from what was
an inevitable drift toward ever-new hours

If only I could imprison the past
within me
set free bad feelings
never to be heard from again
take just our love and
fire the kiln
then melt them down
into just one day
I can keep
an eternal now
so I feel you
still within me
an ember
shedding heat
into each living cell
even as I disappear
into my future
and you remain wooden
a distorted glowing effigy
of our best days

ocean waves cross skin
bright coral blossoms under eyelids after cloud
clears
a breeze brushes away excess heat
this "before" a lazy unframed sketch
before deeper pleasures
before pain
before the realization
she will love me
or the moment I accept
she will not
before sunhat gorgeous
before sunglasses eyes
before cotton willowy and wispy sundress
a plaything to breeze
her eyes and body a mystery
inside unwritten lines

before eyes first meet
the sound of a car engine's last turn
the feathery vibration of key sliding from ignition
air leaving lungs after a journey
from everywhere to
a tiny chamber inside
a sigh
the next moment is still ink
her mind unpapered
undecided or fervently resolved

shall I rest the pen
or continue these hopeful lines
without accepting the past
and ignore
what it means
to turn a page?

Air softly caresses the couple's intimate mouths
their promises the notes
of a love song with sensuous stanzas

Stars blossom
made viscous by fog
which slips upon the altar
by a lake
All is now still
save water's lapping waves
ever grasping at the shore

The lovers begin to dance
wordless
invisible
shrouded in a mist
whose petals open and close as they sway
in perfect grace
two punky kids from sinkhole nowhere
and strip mall futures
cheeks touching, tears kissing and falling
together
ever down
as one

You cannot feel me
inside our almost embrace
My soft hook arms
more gentle than sighs
end at fingers
like butterflies hovering over skin
we are each cushioned in air
breakable
unbroken

You cannot see me
my eyes failing dams
whose silent tears are planted on cheeks
each drop a tiny flag
of surrender

You cannot hear me
for speaking
would cheapen air
outside your mouth
and I would lose the chance
to listen
as your breathing shallows
the push and pull of lungs
like a slow dance inside

we begin to sway
in time
to heartbeats
synchronized

Will you know me?
My hope is nestled in lips
sliding backward into view
ear, then brow
mouth
You look into my eyes
I have silently asked you a question
my face is nearing yours
our stare unsustainable
the air about to be broken

a new moon is beautiful because she is always beautiful
wedding a handsome sky
under cerulean veil

she descends from the altar of day and exits to rice
thrown in the shape of stars
a bride
pulling tides
tugging everything
even time
even you:
invisible behind doors
with gossamer gravity
you are always beautiful too
throwing heat and light
in equal measure
full of dawns
the glow of your wishes rising
to action

you are like a beautiful sun
wedding a handsome sky
and I, the living earth
ever drawn
while endlessly falling
for you

You Are My Almost

the room is asleep
and time is a monolithic river
passing
as we lay parallel
two lines almost touching
each alone in unconsciousness
hovering in separate lands
unaware of the two-bodied bed
you are my almost

I wander timeless through alternate night
a reading
by mumblers in a hurricane

running
though wanting to fly
my wings
become a ladder
I climb to you
we leap
then blackness
as I am caressed by half-sleep
aware of closed eyelids
and ears
married to the sound of your breathing
I want this moment
to last forever
if only so we can be together that long

love is perfect and eternal in its promise
before it becomes real
less is possible than in a dream
but if lucky
it is infinitely better

you are my all
and I move to embrace you
across a river
two lines intersecting
then merging
into one

I break into a smile on seeing you
and the moonlight of that moment
reaches you before I have taken a second step
A midday kiss begins, deep and unending,
while the sun
its fuel fusing
burns light through sky
at the speed of light
our lips seeking more than lips
hands pressing and sliding along flesh
first button sought and undone
and still we are sunlit from minutes before
hand pulling hand inside
shades drawn
falling into each other
brightness
growing inside
with our impending consummation
sunlight falling harmlessly outside as we
burst and incinerate then
quenched of flames and smoldering in half sleep
talk about this moment
we are in love
that shall live for a million years
each star in its own time
bending in the air
and landing here for upturned eyes
every twinkle at that moment
a wink at the ones
who follow

The universe took a snapshot
across eternity
the day our love was perfected
and sent it
in two-hundred billion trillion tiny white lights
so everyone could
share

29

Darn

shall I measure our time in socks?
new on first date
when we walked for hours
learning to be together
my feet sanded and aching as if socks had not
been broken in
socks are a stupid way to measure our love
perhaps better is the incremental loss of anticipation
in the moments before dates
because we so frequently meet
or the diminishing possibility of sharing any still unknown part of
each other
our lives mutually retained
and our time more like two comfortable shoes
no
shoes are ornaments for burials
polished for everyone but us
their leather outlasting the feet inside
no
this love
our love
is the socks that last until they don't
like cushions against the day
re-cleaned, softened and intimately grasping skin
malleable, snug and always there
and when finally a hole appears
inevitably small
it is darned
like old friends and lovers patching things up
and fitting better than when we first met

This is a jazzy number about
an uptown subway line

We slid 12:30 AM
into a concrete underground blue-green-glare fluorescent funhouse
with a closing time dancehall
stickup vibe
the other pretty people onto pretty things
and we're the only ones
who see the fun
in traveling here
I feel the air's gentle pressure
from furtive glances
Who sees an opportunity in us?
Who is looking to do the dance
shift the feet and swing the hands
that might lead to
a score?
we're too cool for games
and paired up already
and so we dig the music of the C train's wheels
scratching and shaking the floor then
laying a groove on the fade

you are thinking people die here
I can see it in your eyes
and my smile is a Keep Out sign
like I'm in a panic room
and you're cornered on the other side
but I can read a room
and even the incoherent mumbler leaning toward us ain't nothing
but a harmless proposition

we made the system
to protect us
that is why we can sway and tap the night out
to a pianist's deep Berlin beats
and blow off the line of posers needing Ubers
and their disinfectant tires scrubbing the city clean
there ain't no beat in the roll, man
so we descend to the A
just for the realness of the ride

31

There is a fine silt settling over the sidewalk and street
an invisible poison
gunpowder and shrapnel filling breaths
The air is infected
My clothes dusted with disease
and I love her
and miss her and my door is an airlock
sealed tight against everything
bad in this world
and good

If I could stay here forever
I might make it out alive
and miss her and love her too much

but
I can rip off the door seals
Hold my breath and
Free fall to her
A blossoming cloud in my wake
Choked with every germ and virus
cremated by love
and missing her

Me
At her door
I live for her and I am
at her door
and yet
She may have a gun in her mouth
And I must knock
and yet
I might have a gun in my mouth, too
and yet

One cannot understand love
nor its direction
from high school classes
a study list of its characteristics
homework or
pop quiz
or life

It is dormant or dominant
Sating and insatiable
Cruel in its sleep and its rages
and beneficent
But these are just words
their meaning revealed too late to prevent heartbreak

This generation has its own Romeos and Juliets:
thoughtful, shy
flirting and passionate
expressing well-grooved
doubts and desires
They will outgrow the role like those before
in an eternally rolling season of new love

They download apps
onto their phones
all swiping east
and drowning in the abundance
hoping the algorithm is skewed for them
and that matches are waiting just outside of view
with good looks and engaging asides

each of them a piece of candy
staring at an endless conveyor belt of candies
searching for the one who will see them as sun
or an irresistible sweet

Dating in the Modern Age

we are prompted
to use travel destinations as signifier
like a few chunks of rock from which
a good scientist can extrapolate
a place
its land temperate or extreme
the soil hospitable for growth or
spent and fallow

am I to be known by favorite season or sport?
by beaches, mountains or great cities?
by multiple choice keystrokes from which one decides I now
know this place? I like this place? I choose it?
And you swipe and we meet
and the rocks are nothing like me
you get lost in my Paris streets and
no longer understand Paris
you huddle for cover and are bored to death in my war-time Baghdad
the city an unknowable fever and stolen sleeps
and the beach and mountains such interior journeys
landscapes seem merely shells to the me inside
and you are left to throw away the rocks
the maps
and explore me
or move on to someone whose answer
is the entire planet you seek

I like romance
and long walks
Someone with a sense of humor
who knows how to take a joke
unblemished with a willingness to get tattoos

Seeking a partner who loves when I smile
and knows every embrace is earned
Height does not matter
though if you're under 5' 8" be beautiful
(assuming that's even possible)

I seek a premier athlete
(endorsement deals drive me wild!)
I respond to
a social media presence with more than a million followers
in case we need to get the word out!
Must accept criticism and subtle manipulation
I find it validating
I am a giving partner:
make me happy and I'll make you relieved
Most important of all
I seek honesty
well not really but if you believe me
then I might want to meet you

The After

Our loss of contact
is a scar I shall always bear
so invisibly slender
as to be forgotten
Except for an ache
when the pressure dips
rain is imminent
I touch my heart
and run an index finger along the misshapen skin
a forever reminder of loss that runs across me
like a raised river
never spilling out

She wanted an intelligent conversation
for once in her life
But what is intelligence?
Is it found in the ways we thrive best when we are kind
or in how we eliminate threats, human and otherwise?
Shall I speak of profits and genesis of innovations
or of the benefit of suffering now for the others who follow?
Or perhaps the arts and of spelunking in the depths of spirit to better
sense the amorphous soul?
Or discourse on the arcs of science and math, of logic and tested
paradigms?
Is it most ravishing in one's command of the arcane
or in the breadth of what one can know, though scarcely sinking past
surface?
Does command come from intimate bond with the encyclopedic past,
knowing today, or in intuiting
what's next?
Shall I unleash a taut formula like Einstein's
that will take a lifetime to explain
or weave tall tales like Scheherazade to enlighten, engage and
entertain?
I don't know.

She was tired of online videos showing rooms
filled with dominoes
of cats and the way they weave around toilet paper centers
was finished with the easily debunked dunces
those people whose lies inspire others into streets
was tired of the endless anger

and how everyone
knows
everything

The very definition of intelligence.

Pause the video near the end
before the last domino falls
or the steel ball has rolled down the inverted snowboard
and into the funnel
and ask yourself
What is the point?

The past only matters
in how it impacts today
inspiring effort or surrender
knowing optimal outcomes
are always unlikely

Now consider the end zone
after a long drive across the field
if you're on the opposing team failing to stop it?
What is the college degree
after years of learning and tests and understanding
to those who never finished?
the wedding certificate
after the years of love and easy devotion, disagreements, compromise
and divorce?
Viewers watch for the last domino
and see failure if it is left standing

What could be worth
all the effort?

The effort
The effort it inspires
(and the thing the effort makes
and sometimes topples)

Our first call, remember?
Sunset rolled through picture windows
a threaded beam
of 95-million miles
stopping
on your face
and the hand-sized framed photograph
of tiny girl
posing in skates on pond
stumbly legs and feet frozen
in perfect seeming ease
before her fall

Your eyes stray
The light and pull
of sun and daughter
cohering across time
into newly fresh and ancient feelings
of love at her fear
and fear at your love

Two towns away
sudden night spreads
sun rays bending at the gravity of your glance
into the picture
the rest of your room a starless black sky
Your feelings
brightening the last feet of light's journey to her
frozen on ice
through time

Your love and fear
Are light and gravity
two states of existence
sharing an equals sign
The past never leaves you
The present is already past
The future never arrives
And it's you and her and always

Losing A Great Love

The day is a hammer
Glass panes smashed with hard light
thundercracks shatter the hovering air
and sheets of frigid rain boil
on melted oven streets
steam peeling roofs and rooms
a chilled downpoured shirt plasters
sweaty skin
Everything is wrong

The night is made of feathers
tapered at the edges
to smooth the flight toward darkness
but the cushioning air
breaks apart
all the way
to ground
and scatters
in mournful monotone waves

a single, short questioning honk as faint as a whisper
is answered by the sound of
distant tires receding
like the last sigh of a love
sinking
in a never ending ocean
of sighs

Before the Big Bang
nothing yet united
She backs away to pull me in
from streetlamp's false dawn
She is the tugging ache that honors my longing

She says everything is connected
I pull at tissue paper constructions
inside each candy box conspiracy

Her confident eyes are as beautiful
As the sounds slipping red mouth

I am as gentle and meaningless
As she
She wants me
Singularity

It is dawning and dark
Entropy

Assassination Talk

I am constantly firing bullets with my words
that I had thought were "hello" and "let's work it out"

only to watch others stagger back
pull guns and aim for my heart

I die every day
and after I fall
in those final moments
breathing shallow and vision dim
my last feeling
is of bewilderment
re-playing the moment
to learn how I was
so misunderstood
and at least point out the error
before I'm gone
It seems stupid to go down for a misperception
infinitely sad to be done in
and never know why

yet now I notice
when someone's harmless greeting seems suspect
that I am angered
and I snap
like there is no choice
but to shoot first
and kill with words
over nothing
more than "hello" and "let's work it out"

Lullaby

I observe you
moving through wind
willing cold muscles and bones
ever forward on an efficient trajectory
lifting legs over granite chunks
and up the brown leaf-carpeted incline
through thin unmarked woods
in search of an overhang where we can stop
and wait for the rain to end

I follow you closely
in the calm draft of your sheltering body
safe
aligned to the cuddling rhythm of your steps
like the rocking of a baby in a mother's arms
regular and sweet

Today I learned the value
of getting lost
and of panic
and shouting until my throat hurt
I learned about
the benefits of giving up and
waiting to die
and how to dread no one is coming to save us

I learned how to make bad decisions
how to edge another person in the direction of death
and how to cry until I cannot breathe

You learned you were willing to die
to save me
and to be still
long enough
to appreciate the speed sunlight can
succumb to rainclouds
and day to dusk
to love how the world really works
while I learn enough
to try to survive

maybe soon we can stop
the land will dry

you will light a fire to smoke the sky
we will find water
ration what food we have left
and I will learn to accept
the world that is
not yet ready
to let us go

To know is to see

The sun
underneath the forest dark
slowly thrusts itself toward higher ground
hidden behind a city of trees
invisible stars fading
a purple and orange bruise
at the imagined edge
a painted herald
declaring the sun's approach
and that we be awakened refreshed
restored to action
and commence the singing of songs
and laughter
that we smile and be warmed at the blessings
of our good fortune

The sun
hurls ever deeper into outer space
away from every other celestial body
at once
dragging us with it:
a corkscrew dog spinning on an invisible leash
as we look down
at the button
we press inside our cage
eager rats
trained to know it is us
who measures and makes the day
we are the ones who press the button
which yields the toys
the love, the prompts and algorithmed suggestions
of what to think

press press press swipe swipe swipe
and the forests and animals and each of us
recede
from each other at once
while in each moment our shadows grow
and fade

a spider on self-belay swings in gentle breeze
the leaves, beyond, shudder and settle
their dark faces plated toward sky
above, clouds spill and roll in air
my impatient eyes unwilling to watch them change

what am I to learn?
the spider's hunger inspires the making of thread
leaves only dance when blown
clouds are airy playthings of
sun, geography, winds, humidity, gravity, temperature

and the world within me?
in methodical analysis of my line of sight
the most incomprehensible of all

It is For You

To be the one who gives comfort
Whose words undo affliction
cause the angry to lay down arms
and bring clarity about the misunderstood

To grace a gauntlet of pilgrims
whose sleepwalk-sluggish fingers
are the answer
to an invitation of touch

Unbranded
unaffiliated
unknown except in words
and actions
unsellable
with value unlinkable to exploitation
offering relief
and the peace that follows
mutual surrender

Jesus asked a peasant the way
but was thought too much trouble
Lincoln asked a clerk to join his practice
but was unworthy of a man on the go
James Dean, parking lot attendant
asked out the prettiest girl at CBS
who preferred movie star handsome
Easy choices all
one poor, one awkward, one slight
these young men no match for anyone
the nobodies others avoided
until history said
yes to them and
we lived or thrived in their wake

three refused them:
a peasant, a clerk and young lady
each with
better things to do
none of them ever knowing
whether the trajectories of those men
might have lit our lives far longer
or less had they said yes

a confession:
every bobsled-turn flight over fires
every epic superstar water drop
over blow-ups and blowbacks
is preceded by a
preventable conflagration
a brief flash
that nature nurses
to a headline-only disaster
no font size large enough to capture scale

I quite enjoy the chance
to be the hero
and while I would never be author to any horrors
I would be different without them:
just a guy whose life
was full of other things

If I were to have spotted the match
a moment early
the wrist bent at an angle
a sulfur tip poised to scratch
across red phosphorous and glass
I hope I'd flick that match from eager hand
and disappear
the forest cool in springtime breeze
the morning normal in every way
one unlightable match that could have made a hero
but made a nobody
who saved the day
better than ever before

I did this
I did that then more of this and that and
then other stuff and this other stuff
and wondered how I could ever get to
this this this and that
that other stuff
and then this?
got in my car
went here then there
to do other stuff and more of this and that
got into my car
and did other stuff while I
went from there to there and got stuff
while I did stuff
went there and then here
and did small stuff and big stuff
and wished I got more done
but it was time for that
I did that until morning
and then I did this

Life

When it could not get worse
a disaster loomed
with no way out
it was hopeless
a brick wall
the end was near
up a creek
effort was futile
escape was impossible
a lost cause
just a matter of time
the hammer was about to fall

Then just like that
in an instant
a new day
a corner turned
a light at the end of the tunnel
out of nowhere
when least expected
fortune smiled
the skies cleared
and I knew
it would be fine

Primal Scream

I have no idea as to the breed of dog
I'm limited to common college rites:
the slow methodical hours of study
the ongoing pursuit of degree and girls
and conventional interior glides
from liquids fermented and distilled

the dog was big and I would ride
fifteen miles on the bike for a haircut
then return before lunch was over
and a class begun

shorn and five miles back and
midwest suburb and a dog
lion barking and I look
up a hilled lawn to house
because those are primal screams
at me
and my glance is ignition
to his muscles

the dog in a blur of flesh and bark and missile plume
parallel to me
down the hill
I accelerate and burn He's even faster
I keep edging past what I had thought
was maximum effort
he jets across sidewalk to curb
he's going to come for my legs to pull me down
I primal scream
and I will make sure he dies
before I bleed out
he careens into the street
the distance closing to
next to nothing
and then a whoosh
and stuttering
a dog a car
the sound of no one in pursuit
me
faster
at last
alive

Miraculous

Later
no one will need to keep sharing the way
they chose to pull together
and made peace with each other
planted
conserved
preserved
turned everything around

They will always remember where they were
when success was assured
and who called them to help absorb the news
that they could remain alive after all
because it was too much
to process alone
What does it even mean when no one dies needlessly?

They will recall their anxiousness
when the phone lines jammed
and each of them was isolated and unreachable
for the first time in their lives
the way their hearts raced, breath quickened
and dread came alive inside
with a shiver
This might be the moment everything falls apart

They will always remember us, too
We are the ones who are choosing
to make their survival
miraculous

There is a fence around this place
but only for us
in this land of quarterlife and death
of friend in middle school gunned down
we honor her with candles we got at dollar stores
from money earned in after school jobs

Her name
she had a name
and she would laugh about anything
we all liked her
But everywhere is the wrong place and
always is the wrong time
and that's where she was when she was

Those candles
some old film crew white guy
seeing only expiration date
starts to pull them
our urban glass black charred daisies unscripted
in someone's stroll through
a scene
him killing her a second time
her memory
worth less than

EXT. A GRITTY BACKGROUND - DAY

We came at him
for her
but there were more of them
and they were white
and would make things bad
Her name
she had a name
he apologized
they promised to put them back
all they got was their shot
and they left
but we got
the chance to hear her laugh
and to lose her always

no matter how unalike in character
from radical, electric and booze infused
to contemplative and dreamy in temple
or elegant with tuxedoed and gowned players
every concert
demands of the listener
a performance of rituals

it begins with a traditional exchange of alms and invitation
next
on the day appointed
one honors trained presenters
with timely arrival
to be then escorted or otherwise directed
where to witness the presentation
there is to be a processional upon a stage
and an acknowledgment of the presenters by the gathered
who shall ritually slap hands in unique tempos
unless all are anxious for the ceremony to begin
when one may slap hands at regular intervals
in unison with others

the service is performed
hands slapped when presenters pause

in the ceremony
melodies are fuel
set alight in ears
a firestorm of wonder and excitement
exploding inside
heroes and innocents may be sacrificed or saved
love found or lost
longing, exultation and regret
intermingling
the music is to
make one fully alive and better
ideal, really

then one shall slap hands, leave
and remember

If this first line is a temple door
an invitation to enter
a sacred space
and this fourth line a pew
to walk past while in contemplation
accept this promise of certainty:
If you read as far as here
near the front
then sit
you will find
your way to a better life
worthy of a lifetime of time
fully aware
that we need you

Take these as offerings:
You are not yet great
Yet full of goodness
changing the world for better
and ill
with all you do
Acquire knowledge through study
and contemplation
Only those who see all sides
can recognize the right side

The feeling of greatest fulfillment is yours
when the most selfless act
becomes your most selfish desire

You shall re-enter the world
in five lines
ready to become authentic
Know that someone
is thinking of you now
full of hope and affection

I stop writing
proofread
publish

What is worthy of
your taking to the streets?
Or the kind of affection to make you rush into someone's arms and say
you never felt so much?
What words would you use to twist into a knife
or mold as a bandage to wrap a wound and stop the bleeding?
What manifesto of yours is so buoyant and wide you could
hold it overhead to catch the wind and fly?
Or so destructive as to lob stanzas like grenades
until the page was empty and the battle won?

This poem has value
like all examined lives
True, you won't read this and silently thank me
for insights
The title is a question
I have answered with questions
But I didn't write this work.
You will.

Henrik Ibsen's "An Enemy of the People"
was on
the news
something about a doctor's warning and a mayor
who wanted to plow on
people could die, the doctor said, but really what else was new?
still the hamlet will be indecisive about it
quite a battle those two started but we need to survive
keep the money flowing
so we can buy caskets and gravestones
and pay the pastors to sigh and praise
the good and faithful lives of my
son
my daughter
my father
my mother
my neighbors
and so many strangers I never will know
righteous sermons on how God took them too soon
but He is wise and knows
what He is doing
we will fill the church with love
wail on the shoulders of those who remain
and pray
that arrogant, insufferable doctor will just lay off
and we can get back to work
it's a miracle God hasn't taken him
but martyred us instead

weeks since sun knew my face
i emerge squinting
unrecognized but politely welcomed
with gentle warmth and an amber bath from
the dying sun
and in every direction i choose to look
people
are back walking and pushing strollers
spilling out from restaurants and bars
waving, living
finally and kissing and laughing
with everyone
they love most
all at once
as if nothing
had
ever
happened
or would
i want to scream
of a plague
they know is here
put my mask on
and stagger home
reeling from the threat of connections
while love is on its murderous rampage
and the people we live for
we can willingly die for
rather than compromise a single moment more

the night is dark
everyone can see what they want
secure they hear everything
as a silent wave
sweeps through

Communism in Action

From him according to his lack of ability
To him according to
his need for absolute domination
and to find a weakness in everyone
to lie and see if you note it
your feeling his rot and squirming in filth until
the moment you smile or nod
and you are lost

he needs to wake up to the world waking up
to him
jealous of him, debating about him, arguing for him and
praising him like a funhouse mirror version
(nine feet tall)
until he is an infallible man
a real man with a working heart, the best heart
and new clothes like an emperor's
only real women can appreciate its cobweb
weave
all must envy his beauty
and tell him so
like his life depends on it

but he always needs just one more compliment
to survive
and a coronation worthy of Stalin

stories
are a forensic tool making plain our ascent
and decline
first presenting
as grunts and rhythmic taps
evolving into symphonic odes and tender sonnets
scented with nuance
words composed amidst oceans and mountain air
a consonance of nature's gentle hands
and considered insight
in lyrical harmony

then a climb to the very peak of passion
with one-facet heroes
and justified cause
battle-cry wars and bottomless regrets
of steep dissolution and clanked metres that
jut at unnatural angles
madness and knives
and cliff faces with no next
ropes of liquid hemlock
to destroy climbers before
and after
the fall

to chaos
toasted in a cafe somewhere
at the raw edge where coffee and whiskey
help busy a last few tiny mouths to silence
empty streets at the bottom of the ocean
of ever warming air
lined with windows
lit by an audience of screens
for which fingers pass on our status
with emojis
like, 'ya know, grunts and rhythmic whatever
¯_(ツ)_/¯

i.

When did I last think of
the sands of Africa?
of the wind's hurried journey across land
carrying native grains
each subsequent breeze a new resolve
to force them
to the river and
downriver to the sea
carried by currents across an ocean
each grain smashed and broken
some of what's left is here
on this tiny part of beach
your feet shortly to slip out
as you fall
a journey as natural as skin

ii.

[text omitted at request of author]

iii.

My family were enslavers
it's in a book a relative thought to write
my blood branded with
a permanent stain
I am chained to
the shameful inescapable past
Are we connected?
Two families on opposite ends of the ocean
then across an auction block?

iv.

it is not enough to catch you
though I do
barely
it is not enough to
apologize for not seeing you
though I do
barely
it is not enough to
offer to help you up
though I do
barely

62

it is not enough to
want to know you
though I do
fervently
as if you are the blessing
and I the sins
as if you are the answer
and I the silence
as if I can never escape the rotting plantation
my stupid family made
and you are free

v.
When had I last thought of the book
Or of the great uncle who needed to know?
Was it meant to be trophy?
A playbook?
An apologist's scroll?
A mere restoration of playing cards into
preferred order?

vi.
We don't play with unstacked decks
We explode them
And people die
And nature is also harsh and unrelenting but
Always pushing and pulling us into opportunities
to catch every card
Instead we are the wind
We blow until they fall
and claim
There are no good cards left
Here is a poem
All about me
I'm sorry
[text omitted at request of author].

Who (Anger is Another Word for Fear)

who grabs her son and stands on a corner
saying "no more"
hands at sides
sidewalk pushing
against feet
the sky gaping
in an infinite roar she can hear in her head

who raises a fist in the air
her brow bent in a V at the enormity
of everything wrong and those infinitely wronged

who marches to the front of the line
just inches from officer
and freezes
she's reached the moment now
this is the center of the world and it's his turn
dare her to do something
because then she will do everything
holding his gaze like it is a rope and she will
never let go until she pulls him to her side

who ties a rope into a noose
who grabs gun and chases a jogger
who kneels on neck
who chokes a human to death because
loose cigarettes
but really
the veiled threat
the promise the others made each other (others?)
the obvious undeniable truth (is it really?)
that the others are
coming for everyone we love (they are?)
and everything we ever had (you actually believe this?)
and the best we can do (this is really the best you can do?)
is push that day to tomorrow (are you sure that push isn't a pull?)

who holds the hands of strangers
who takes a knee for justice
who promises to break up an attack so all might share and be kind
in the naive hope she won't die for the cause

who is willing to kill for the cause

64

like murder is on a straight line he can move down to win
but it's just a merry-go-round
we are all just pushing and pulling
making it ever faster until we can't hang on when all we need to do
is
to
make
it
stop

When

The officer's hand still an inch from his handgun
The young man's hands still in the air
The guy walking by, the guy with the cellphone recording
nothing special

The young man's father still waiting for him around the corner

The officer's wife moving her finger toward blue button
to Confirm Payment
for sleepaway camp
at last
their first time alone
since kids were born

The woman who will be struck down in a week
while giving voice to her fear
opening her mouth to say yes and thank you to
six consecutive double shifts

The baby child who will grasp a burning flag with tiny hands
then be identified
threatened with assassination
and sent into hiding
writing answer to three plus five and waiting
to feel the gentle squeeze of her mama's hand when she is done.

The protestors, officers, reporters, the artists
passersby, coroner, historians and great, great grandchildren
The cop, the kid, the dad, the wife, the child
all of us
in a life
ticking like a clock
eternally forward
at only one speed
everyone trying to get to a good place
a better place
a moment at a time
second
by second
We all just wanted to slide through this day
like all the others
It was a matter of time
tick

Thinking is a switch turned on
hell, it takes microvolts inside your skull
chemical reactions sent down pipes in the attic
and you figure the who
figure the why the where the when
but that ain't nothin'
just a tiny hit of power
still feels good don't it
swimming in that happy blood bath
feels good to be this angry don't it
to forget the worries
but you are just so totally harmless
and worried

Raising a hand
is a second switch turned on
a call to action
a What am I doing?
like making a revolution or killing someone
a Something
and you feel ready
don't you?
Like maybe it is
the time to act
Hoping you see it through
legs torso ears eyes arms weapon going together
in a quickening blur of slow motion
you're righteous, right
lost and tight
and it feels so good
that nothing else matters

Except everything matters

How

ashes, sparks and bright embers
scar air and streak
in graceful arcs
deadly beautiful talons
branding skin with owner's marks
so abundant as to burn and rot us red
dancing on the glowing ground
our apartment windows blown out
roofs heat-crusted
bare feet dripping with the blood
of everyone we have ever known

a second wish would take too much time
we're fully alive
the only moment
terror
we cannot feel more terror but are force fed
terror constantly bloated bursting
every feeling
no
reason
matters
it is always twilight
I have no plan
no stopping here
alone and slicing torso
through a furnace this is no life
this is my life

if only there was
a way
I would spread my
arms
gird you
and we could run away
in each other

The question
Why?
when cast
is an adamantine chain
toward answers

even love
is less
made of belief
promises and
queries for reasons to exist (why?)

Why?
is the combination lock on a safe
holding maps
to who we are
that few ever see
and none see all
Each holds paths, cliffs and caves
dead ends, dead bolts, keys and clear-eyed summits
destinations become unexpected trailheads
that inspire new: "Whys?"

Why?
is the enemy to
every wrong
and reason we despair and stop
and fail to find relief

The right answer too rarely
precedes the "why"
"That is why" is a blunt billy club
following wishes presented as conclusive evidence
often saddled with an adamantine chain
to new questions
unshackled from good answers

Every Day is Unfinished

before the nomenclature
the PTSD, ASD and RAD
was a time of dancing
in the chaos of nuance and ambiguity
wildly unsure
of the landscape of mind
knowing the agony, confusion and utter madness of
misinterpreting something newly noted and uncharted
when improvisation meant blowing things up
in people whose lives were big and hopeful and dreadful
mysterious and terrifying but it most mattered to explorers
that we were unmapped
like Van Gogh in front of mostly white canvas
not yet haunted with the indigo sky
but the amber and gold of harvest solved and pressing on him to
continue
the prismatic colors of loss he will mix and scrape into a
monochromatic muddy pupil and iris
a brown stroke of hat
blackened green on soaring Cypress
all he sees
acquiescing to his stubborn brush and knife
thrust inside a work of calm, tortured, ravishing beauty

Today we signed paperwork and met deadlines
went home and left it all
behind
We are finished
and in the evening
at home
we fire up some screens
and vegetate
secure that the big mysteries are solved
we are unhaunted
we can name everything
and enjoy the benefits of understanding
nothing

We Will Tuck Inside Our Skin and Call Us

We rage
We sputter
We try to love endlessly if we are lucky
or yearn hard and long
smash against our edges
even at risk of ripping flesh
in search of
something new
we will tuck inside our skin and call
Us
but we always feel the same
this drifting
stuck in our heads
floating in unimportance
measured and bordered
and bored

and so We rage
We sputter
We try to love endlessly if we are lucky
or yearn hard and long
smash against our edges
even at risk of ripping flesh
in search of
something new

71

ii.
it's going to get insane again
it's nuts now
everything is terrible
and we can't imagine
how to feel anything not tied to dread
if only we had read more we might
know what to do
or if we possessed a quality made for this day
something that we decided
set us apart
but this moment seems made for others
we are fighters that cannot be blessed nor battled
mere dreams
with endless opportunities we could seize
if only we thought we were unique

i.
every reason that has driven a person to ruin
or to heights unimagined
every act that makes waking hours
the stuff of dreams and nightmares
with rising skies, marble legs astride battlefields
newly won acres under planted flag
or filled with dead friends
each resignation, graduation and next endeavor
everyone and every corner of this earth
is unique
on an infinite line of unique events
road mapped and training manualed
made cautionary tales in history books
so we can be properly prepared*

*history tells us only
what others were capable of before

They Are Responsible

We are known for complaining together
with all who agree
While others march
donate
work the jobs and do the research
run for office
cut the deals
build organizations
sacrifice carefree hours to work
lose sleep
lose friends
lose love
and make the future
I dread

I blame them for depravity
For savage and unrelenting blitzkriegs against
goodness
and all the bad they can do in the world

For which we are responsible

We made ourselves
for different lives
which got away
overtaken by easier fictions
that subsumed our preferred natures
and revealed the handicaps
of such casual
virtues and flaws

we become
who we never planned to be:
shortsighted and opinionated
regretful of what we can't have
navigating our stories to fit the era
and padding them with fantasies
to render us small and therefore
blameless

When leaders exhort us
we can become pawns
if we choose
Only when we behave
can they fully believe
they have lives that matter

We made ourselves
to be better
there is time
to see it through
or to slither behind
circumstances
and become shadows
insignificant
parts of something
gargantuan

Someone had to be Martin Luther King, Jr.
to learn to write
before pen could set
his testament
in the native tongue of ancient kings
Someone had to be King Charles I
divinely ordained to rule foreign lands
executed for claims of absolute rule at home
Someone had to be Stephen Langton
Archbishop of Canterbury daydreaming text for the
Magna Carta
with singular insight and a talent for phrases
unaware his words
would lead to the death of kings
sire a kind of democracy
to grow and spin out for centuries
and so powerfully shape a Georgia preacher's words
a King in a city still unbuilt
on a continent unknown
He had to be the one
to split the Bible into chapters, too
and miss forever his brother Walter, who died
and doubtless affected
his words
Someone has to be you
inheritor of history and
its maker
author, victim, lover, priest, king
setting your testament
in words, thought, influence and precious days
your story shall end
your impact prevail
And someone will have to be the person made
or unmade
by you

History Rhymes

there was a period
between the election and soft ascension to power
between the views the prison-penned struggle made plain
and realization that citizens must treat them as true
there must have been millions of
Germans simply
frustrated
stuck with nothing to do but complain cautiously
frustrated as business had to be re-thought
new accounting and regulations navigated
frustrated at how much harder socializing might become even with
Nazi membership
frustrated at being noticed too much
and the fanatics and militias wandering the streets
the books burned
But between the initial terror and mild urge to escape
from the Reichstag fire to
Kristallnacht, its immediate aftermath and beyond
there would be no brave acts that saved millions
no anti-Nazi righteousness enflaming anyone but one
to even try
History should note
that when they were called for greatness
and courage
a people rose
to impatience at the inconvenience

Crossing the Rubicon

Legio XIII masses at the edge of a shallow January river
but really a stream
as a lone figure
squeezes his horse's sides

two teens in love with boyfriends
alone on the shore
sip soda they spiked
only noticing each other
as a passenger jet slowly paints a plume across the sky
they stare and dare each other to disrobe

a mother in medieval grass
with legs open
a baby girl emerges and takes a frosty breath

heroin high gone
a toothless gnome ambles from under ancient aqueduct
in slippery search through mud
her sister unaware they are walking toward
each other
desperate to give up

a CEO in a Fiat
listening to Madonna as she approaches the bridge
singing and posing with her free hand
as steering hand drifts

a young woman on all fours
frantically searching for glasses in thin waters
as soldiers approach

a riverside woman reading Plato
as light fills afternoon trees
the shadows dancing and alive
her nodding yes and understanding so much more
the shadows' very source
she records it on parchment
rapturous
removes shoes and stockings
grasps newly scribbled words and footwear above the slow water
and crosses

Utopia

some of us will choose a leader
to be blamed or adorned with garlands
four years of our diminishing lives will ride on the choice
one a person of vision
with the right temperament for these times
the others, painfully
not

a number of us believe all candidates are equally bad
or that elections don't matter since there is a grand conspiracy
to pre-ordain a victor
a few preach we can become perfect if we renounce
what worked and failed
then aim at the highest of pleasures and cooperation
reliant only on good will
It will end, it always does eventually
but
next time can be different, they will say
and maybe it will be for awhile
each day better for the effort

While all movements will be defeated
all lives end in death
what is sought
is what is forever possible
and impossible forever

Robert Frost long fretted at the fork
in the road
Yogi Berra took it

Barista's Lament

It is the barista's lament
that every interaction is a set
of pre-determined questions and answers
a scrawny decision tree of possibilities
Can I take your order size style to go whole skim soy name
I am an old dog on a leash
still aware of everything I want to ask you and share
a movie I saw and my gut feeling we have
a similar yearning for surprise
the fashionista hat you wore last week and your runny makeup today
you have the kindest smile
but I am choked out of me
my leash loose
because I stay inside the lines
thank you for the tip
wait over there for espresso-based
parting words for a stranger
next customer

I love the risk of the rest of the world
At that first step onto sidewalk
a thumb presses snap
opens the hook and drops leash
my collar is unconnected
and I am free to be
unscripted

We are sure this must be true:
A newborn's incessant needs
its squirming and irregular sleeps
must add to the mass of the earth
past the point new parents
ever sensitive
can feel the increased gravitational pull on flesh

And this:
certain overnight infant cries contain clouds
of invisible abrasives
synchronized at perfect opposition to the
harmonious frequency of skin
aching exhausted ears
capable of transforming the tearful expression of a baby
from plea for
loving support
into a threat to unravel
any unsleepable mind
long exposed

There is a hidden exultation
recessive in us from birth
until childbirth
when a gene flips us
away from our long childhood
and to
our reign

after a life of listening
we can finally speak first
transformed into knowing better
we are the smart ones
now unleashed
to do the worst thing ever done to us:
We teach children
to believe adults
understand how things work
though we know
almost any child
can see we don't

This is normalcy
coded
I'm bent over another dead victim
not giving up

This is normalcy
dinner and reality television

This is normalcy
my friends are honest
my enemies lie

This is normalcy
we should sleep
better yet, let's kiss

This is normalcy
security gate small talk, White House
the president's briefing at 10

This is normalcy
Don't mind the bombs

This is normalcy
I'm sick
but the reality is
I need money

This is normalcy
These are not normal times

This is normalcy
listen! her first breath
we'll name her Hope.

This is normalcy
the victim survived

We are alike in vigilance against threats and need for rest
thinking only of our own
and others whose stories
resonate

a cat in Istanbul impassive
under concrete chunk at dawn construction site
the smell of spray paint, human urine and plaster
as animals with yellow colored heads
and clumsy brown feet mew to each other
holding sticks with glowing ends
and blowing smoke from inner fires

she licks a paw and watches as one of the creatures
sees her and points
is she prey or predator?
she crouches but the others make no motion
and after a moment the pointing animal returns attention
to the rest of
the pack
she lowers herself to the ground
and closes her eyes
to sleep

like every sentient life
on earth

You are in a crib looking up at your mother
who is younger than you ever remember
Now you are your mother
reaching down
no word created yet
to describe the amount of love
you feel for this infant
you will invent some to share
you think
because you cannot bear to be alone
in this feeling
while staring into eyes
that will always be yours

You are your partner
succumbing to you
ever falling into a perfect moment
your motion a concise expression of feeling
pressing touches unrelentingly accurate
your body magnetized
and sticking to fingers
invisible stitches deeper than love and making you whole
nerves like fast-opened blinds
overwhelming rooms with sun
a lifetime
re-awakened at once and exploding
outward and in
there should be a word about
this thing that is so much
more than love
because words are necessary in life
to share the imaginable

you as you
telling your mother
you hate her
because you do
uncaring whether this is a phase
or you will always feel this way
your stab sinking inside her
slow inch by slow inch
her love
wasted on an enemy

83

you are your child
at the moment of falling for her first deep crush
she is filled with wonder
struck dumb
for lack of a word about a feeling she thinks
is so much greater than love
that a parent could invent
but has yet to share

a plaid blanket
is spread across grass
stars hide behind the early hour
there is music
to come
everything is possible

We traveled a very long way to get here
after work
through car exhaust
on creeping highways
washed in rolling red waves of brake lights
live reports
of more marches
and leader's tirades
of temperature record
and hotter tomorrow
liquor sales way up
the latest death toll barely mentioned
there is not much new to say
about the era's gasps
you kill the radio
soundtrack to the promises we made to do
something
and just like that
everything is great

the bottle and stemware are pulled
we
the lucky ones
drink

wine

and lie

on a woolen island
in an emerald sea
as heat dissipates
stars twinkle
and the music
begins

There is Always Something (Unsaid)

There was nothing said
One step back, it is over
Two steps and there is no way to prevent
our crash
I travel four steps back and you are perfection
Tourist guide to your sighs like they are each uniquely inspired
Five steps and relief
you
existing with me
One and if only we had never met
Two steps back you say nothing
as we skid
Seven and I am alone in the car
Eight steps back, the car's brakes are going
just like my heart.
Nine, she breaks with me.
Ten steps back she and I head in for the repair.
I stop because she needs to tell me something.
And that is why I met you

Eleven, she holds me.
Twelve, they are slipping.
Thirteen steps back back my brakes work
like ignition, lights, heat, doors, battery, wipers, tires, mirrors
I only notice the things that matter
when they break
Fourteen (I probably love her with all my heart)
she must think I'm indifferent
You do not exist
One step back
(I love you)
Three steps back and I keep driving
silent

she is at war
when she is at rest

offering a neutral expression
under light sweat
as if dreams were innocent, still
and cotton covers
would be armor enough
from the streets
were it not
for his soft pull
and whispered invitations
to snatch the perfumed threads
seeping into unconscious blood
filling her with the unease
that no other promise
matters

soaring relief is her best ecstasy
and she must suffer for it always
unless she breaks with her best lover
the one you can never be
for you cannot make her live that much

her eyes will open
and she will think
like she does every day
of the first time
he made love
him needled inside her
changing chemicals
like a gunner mowing down enemies
it was the only time she had ever known
she could feel safe

Pillowcase Ink and Bleach

the faded stains
made and unmade on pillowcase by ink and bleach
are reminders
like a red patch left after scab
one hopes will heal into skin
and be forgotten

there are too many faults to
remember already
each undoing a migraine that
burrows inside
so many objects rebel and flaw
blowing through the quiet with rages of dents and scratches
ink splattered across the pillowcases of everything
making unclean borders between head and rest
where thoughts should be allowed to lighten
and float away
past caring so much

exhaustion is branded onto every surface
defacements no longer matter
splotchy skin and grey pillows
are a new kind of perfection
in our newly perfect world
of madness and agnosia

My neighbors have taken notice
of the schedule I keep
the Bach and Laura Mvula at all hours
but rather than asking for quiet
or enjoying
great music
one shakes the wall behind bedpost with Diam's
and another at the foot with Radiohead
Per Nørgård from the ceiling
a composer unknown to me
whose slow spiderleg walking progressions unleash in me
my best playlist yet
from the floor Nine Inch Nails'
mesmerizing grooves like sheets of rain
punctuating the Nørgård and making me ecstatic
A campaign for ears
has broken out around me
and it sounds like
Coltranes's Ascension
all of us
geniuses in a complex
inspired by this moment
playing our hearts out
and listening to
what we can make
together
when we feel enough to pound walls
sing with speakers
stomp on floors and share
the music we love most
And when it is impossible to imagine
how it can get any better
the sound of sirens

I have a 10 AM in Conference Room A:
A Performance of What We Should Do
all agreeing to whatever
and singing in unison
to the drums
slammed like a college football cheer beat
on and on and on
like we're drunk fans
after a tailgate
incapable of anything more than
waiting for our cue

11 AM: Slap On The Colors
red ink and bar charts
are armor enough to
protect us from accountants
We grab the paper knives from printer
take the elevators to 8
They think they can write us up
but we thrust and parry presentations until
they are profusely bleeding cash
and forced to retreat by security
with their belongings
resignation letters in hand

12 PM: Taco Tuesday

1 PM Tina in Development
rushes my desk with administrative assistant
staging a coup I knew was coming
I give her admin a promotion
then throw her out
she will land in the mail room
and my new executive assistant calls HR
to post her position

2 PM in Conference Room A:
Make A Bonfire With Accountants' Draft Report
and howl until everyone is laughing
at whatever
then sing in unison
right up to my meeting
with the VP of whatever at 3

This souvenir of nothing
becomes everything
A fifty-year-old testament
to what was possible during a long-forgotten day
Hope has been realized
no
surpassed
inspiring exultation
no
ecstasy
There were the four men in a room who made it
the missing fifth a footnote
no one thinking much about the thing
any more than Picasso thought of the natural strokes
on one canvas among ten thousand works
it was just another
in a long series of anothers
like a step taken
in the middle of a mountain climb
the rock face firm, the foot placed and lifted
experience and muscle memory
reducing the work of the brain to
almost meditative stillness

it is only through reverence that the ordinary becomes animate
Frankenstein corpses litter our past
one lightning bolt away from
making a monster
gloriously alive
again
like never before

Konda (16:29)

Keith spoke first
his piano fingers in an endless loop and lurch of dissonance and
heart rending resolution
skittering shudders of "No!" and acceptance

Aierto's fingers cried across drum skin unrecognizably in all-but-silent
baby welps
as if infinitely pained and
exhausted past the point of sleep
when sleep will not come
eyes welling and
searching for safe haven
until it becomes real
sadness can slip into anger
can become a groove to hide inside

Miles' trumpet cried
and trailed off like
someone had rushed in with news
so shocking and unbearably sad
a few questioning words spilled out of his bell
and then it hit him
there was nothing he would say
and everyone just stared and murmured
He started and went silent
He started and went silent
again and again

All were limited in their grief
in their ability to feel anything
only so much and no more
their piece as much as they were able to make
and no better
the event that inspired the music
only so impactful and just for awhile
everyone filling the end
with their own music
hoping it mattered before it was gone
and then it was gone

A Perfect Delusion of Internal Coherence

Night Seattle bus ride
He wore battle-weary rags rolled above fists like he had one more fight
And I was the misrecognized enemy
who escaped because he didn't have the nerve to finish me off
the first time
his window eyes
cracking at the unforgivable
unawareness in me
as he grinds his squishy brain into
a perfect delusion of internal coherence

I had decided to travel for luxury pasta in distant haunt
and find my way back
To live as prince and pauper
as if entitled to unearned incursions in both lands
but really just ordinary and untouched until the gaunt young man rose
tried to drill his stare through my skull
stepped forward
and pointed outside
I studied every grey cut and smudge on the hard rubber floor
and waited
until my stop arrived
got up and hopped off with a glance
and the youth followed
I think

Where was he?
Orpheus never looked back
entered luxury hotel
still filled with pasta
feeling victimized
while the young man
starved

Me You are doing it now You

But you said
I told you I
Not true you
Here The words you
They mean I
Every time you
Me You are doing it now You
But we're talking about you
That's what you are talking about I'm
I do listen You
Me Why are you
You never accept that I
You never do Never You
You are making this I
You should shut up and I
What I think I

"Every crisis is a decision crisis,"
she said and walked out.

I order a breakfast sandwich with coffee

When someone wrongs me
I get them back
Someone can make a mistake
But no one can make one
twice
Someone in the back is taking too long

I am
sucking in what I sense
unleashing floods of electrical pulses
in a frantic search for understanding
WHAT THE L*#% IS HAPPENING???

"What the l*#% is happening?" I mumble
wait
then the sandwich arrives
made right

If error correction was central to
my survival
I would check how often I was
wrong
or wronged someone
But I'm still here
so for me
I guess it' snot

95

I cannot control my hands.
I rest my finger on the trigger.
I pull out my gun.
I am so winded I am literally shaking.
I push you to the ground.
I run at you with everything I have.
I pull my key to your door insert turn push.
Webern. No one else likes Webern.
I get out of the stairwell on the 32nd floor and careen the hall.
Idiot high rise and I'm taking the stairs.
I drive a thousand miles and pull around the corner.
I put my gun in my jacket pocket.
Even when I try to stand out, no one sees me.
I look so ordinary in this suit. Invisible like always.
I know if I scare you, you will have to take me back.
That isn't good enough, I say.
What, is that Webern ? I shout.
You call me to say you're sorry.
I hate this WEAKNESS.
I cannot go on without you.
I am going to die.
You are the best thing that will ever happen to me.

there is broken glass everywhere
all cupboards emptied at once
in the blankness of arm sweeps and throws
this was work past deadline
a chore that remained like dishes
at the end of a really bad day
this necessary evil
to shatter and splatter everything breakable
as if insides could be made into outside
me become glass
that aches with bursting and disintegration
splintering and exploding in howls
at everyone and everything
until all used up
glass rubble
on exhausted real estate

whoever hardened Pharaoh's heart
could have let him be

I swish bare feet across the floor
pushing shards to the side
like God
parting a parquet sea
no red, thank goodness and
a broom and pan at the wall

I sweep the glass into pan
and raise it
like the lifting of a curse
swing it over the trash
then let it go

In the church of her mind
ex-husband swirled and
manic-swished through
the pus of softening fruit and
and set fire to her effigy
all to an amusement park
calliope
advising the court to hand him everything
and leave her out of it
like always
as she listened to the organ thundering Bach
and prayed

Their daughter
a child still
not squirming
at father's insistence she choose
between them
His pledge: a home where she can play games
and stay up when she wants
"you can count on me
to trust you always
you are an adult like me"

Her ex dancing away
his agreement and
the money he had committed
in court
his very oath
crushed them all with his dime store heels
into pulp on the carpet
oozing with his drool
the sickening perfume of rot
choking everyone there but him
and her

Everyone

I am in every survey
a thin line on a bar graph
of those who survive
of those not robbed
And not abused because of anything

That's me:
Not wronged by unscrupulous scammer
Who did not Click Here for a special deal
Still uninfected
As expected

I am counted
On a better side of the ledger
A statistical counterbalance glossed over
On the way to bad news

Every click of a counter
whether I'd
die to save a drowning person
donate a dollar to a starving stranger
pass from anything but age

A single integer
for every answer
a person
Every One

Two Cones and a Cup

"Two cones and a cup, please?"
My little boy and his crush
sit
so polite and quiet
with twitchy hands under table
being tested as if they might not work right
each head turn
and answer offered
as if with new parts
just off the assembly line
and on the road for a spin
still needing to be
given the chance to open up
and run

I fetch the ice creams
then hands appear and I retreat with cup
the scoops starting to melt
drastic action needed
their focus turned from me
and even each other
to the shiny blonde streaks
of sugar and fat
drizzling down
butterscotch globes
about to go to waste
the race is on
and they laugh and
lick dessert
every muscle
working
while I stir
and nurse
a gloppy soup
and swear
I'll make it up to myself
with a run
tomorrow

boys of a certain age
are reluctant to hug their mothers
an uncomfortable revulsion rises
from the thought of the good and bad of it
neutering their sense
of manners
even the transactional value of such an embrace
is unworthy of effort
leaving mothers
in their hours
to imagine the ghosts of tiny arms around them

overseas over-caffeinated and full of love
under the blue-white lamppost glare in the heat outside
overnight guard shack
a mom lighted
in the middle of a hazy circle slathered on the asphalt
watches a shadow show of bugs
like Keystone Cops piling out
with intentions of saving the damsel on a ledge
but under direction to
flail and run crazy in circles
fall and fail
because that was what they were supposed to do

and while they might not be ideal
they were the reason people
came to the movies
folks might admire the hero and
cheer for the damsel
but they loved the crazy cops

and there they were - her cops
the ghosts of arms moving in every direction
their darkness the shadow
almost visible against the lighted

and

and when my friend begins
a deep lean
his wheels unanchor from mud-slicked asphalt

and when my friend
rescues my eyes with his
from what must be shattered

and when my
friend says how lucky he is
I am there to see him fall

and when
my friend
keeps pleading
like it's his final wish:
we will be friends forever
and there's nothing I can do about it

and
when
he gets back on his bike and rides

I follow

Soupy Me

I keep improvising recipes
of vegetables and meat
Soupy me
mixed this way
by primitive tools
taste buds and addictions
cravings for pepper and corn, heat and salt
coffee and booze
milk the color of bone
morning oatmeal
surface cooled to the texture of skin
somehow stitched and re-stitched together
from the inside
some mad chemist
ripping apart my ingredients
plastering on a new coat of paint
and doing alterations
so incrementally
I don't notice the changes
tinting a strand of hair, adding a wrinkle

All recipes mixed so I can feel
what I had hoped would be happiness
but is instead
the pure satisfaction of scratching
a perennial itch:
the hunger of a hit machine

For the purpose of knowing me
and securing my time on website
hired hands type code
keywords and if-then propositions
customizing content and prompts
to make me efficient
stick to my lane
and play well with others likewise inclined
so when the ads come
we will stay and
we will pay

the pen is a dangerous weapon
because it goes over lines
makes cross-outs and doubles back
proof of the messiness of a mind dragging itself forward
through the mud of counterfactuals
doubts and better arguments
feints and unexpected revelations
the slow exertion of sinking ink on paper
leading to more thoughtful thoughts

the handwritten page is our final flag
raised on high
to salute and honor
the freedom
to think into our better selves

but the blog or vituperative video is more influential
a woman in scrubs
speaks on behalf of a friend:
a nurse on the front lines
bearing witness
to her hospital ward's murder of patients
she says her mother's best friend is dying
because she wore a mask during a pandemic
was near a high tech phone pole
drank water that was insulted and turned black
was felled by God who chose for her to die
her faltering faith an insufficient vaccine

how does one write against the ever shifting wind?
and its currents in which conspiracies float?

and who would work away a life to try to
change one thing
when there is far too much that needs changing?

I pick-up my pen
and write a double rainbow

on the edge of understanding a double rainbow

Perspective
I am falling
outside a plane and yes yes I survived long enough
I fall outside a plane tumbling everything wrong Air
rushes me I
float
And wind
must be blowing from the ground
I see it recede The plane the plane is frozen but must be receding I am
turned up and see the plane the
sky I am looking at sky
I am looking at the horizon Frozen in space wind rushing up The
horizon isn't changing
I am floating
"Pull the chute"
I was looking up at the plane I am looking at the horizon How did I
turn And the wind Will we stop floating and fall
We bounce on rubber band swing
The wind slows.
We float

I hadn't thought to look at the altimeter so I look It doesn't matter now
Did I pull the parachute or did the tandem instructor?
We are a hundred feet up and now now I see us falling falling hit hard

Later I wished I looked straight down
The time after I was seeing unimportant sky before looking at horizon
I erased that turn
I'll never know why we faced the heavens and then
not
Did I pull the parachute?
I was trained to do everything right
He showed me
we practiced
reviewed practiced altimeter 6000 feet pull chute
tap on shoulder and pull chute
who pulls chute?
and the time between facing sky
the plane
and horizon is a question and
I wish I looked at the
ground but
I survived

survived long enough

I work and have friends and family vote do taxes decide what is best
from what I know
That is perspective
do it or
never
pull
the
chute

Fortune Teller

Those who tell the past
are fallible
facts are subject to distortion
misinterpretation, omission and undeserved weight
No one can know enough to know
anything
for sure

We are urged to believe there can be certainty in the future
anchor anchored
at the bottom of a bottomless sea
our fortune the inevitable center
around which the water will be shaped
where chaotic currents shall part in a fixed and predictable way

"Read this," he said
holding paper to my face
and pressed it ever closer until I'd backed against the wall
It seemed a kelp forest of
smudges, grey streams and watery brushstrokes
Nervously, I sank squirming fingertips into skinny jeans
face contorting while I body englished eyeglasses
shrugging
in case guilty of transgressions
against an ancient rite
I imagined him sweeping rigid arm toward the door
and remaining unforgiving statue 'til I leave
"Here," I said to the paper
then squinted through glasses
still not at my ability to focus
"Ah…"

He lowered the paper
and swept rigid arm to the door
"It will all come true."
He remained unforgiving statue 'til I left
My unwritten life read and made fate
to cover part of storefront rent

The register tape at the pharmacy
The speedometer
The clock when I looked
The number of pages in the book I bought
The combined low temperature predictions for this week
My bowling score
The number of incoming emails in each billing period
My last LDL cholesterol number
They are unrelated
Where there should be alignment

The failure to find connections
is an affliction
of my life's incoherence
or my inability to see the truth

I exploded with joy
at the point of recognition
when what the world
was telling me
was revealed
Then it spoke in white noise
insights scrambled by the unknown order of operations

The ability to see
with open eyes
and record information
is knowledge
The ability to recognize patterns
and identify good decisions
is wisdom

Every atom of existence is measurable in numbers
And they will subtract
multiply
divide
and add up to the truth
in me
the moment I find the right pharmacy, car and clock

At the moment of greatest height
How high the cliff only learned too late
the bushy British grass gave way to clay and ledge
slick in the rain
my runner's heavy breath merging with thick fog
the clay invisible a step before

my right shoe slid forward
utterly unexpectedly
toward the sudden sound of waves below
it was the English Channel
I felt a tourist's rush of recognition
at how exotic this was
a predawn run
somewhere in the white soup of Lizard Point
it was romantic
idyllic
my left foot lowered to anchor
in the turf
but my momentum too strong
I was taking a second step
leaning careening to my left
down the clay path

I hit the ground
dusted off the dirt
Everyone falls
when they are infants
adds a neuron or two
and grows up

Centrifugal

Clay
that raw material of earth
wheel-thrown from center
the toe of
a ballerina
moving in perfect circles
her fingers extended
ten graceful weeping willows
flying out in the wind
as she whirls

wet fingers pressing
lip into pout
the toe shifts imperceptibly
clay strafed by outstretched
digits
accidental spout
the dancer leaning mid-twist
gouged side and catching air
arms swinging savagely
like swan necks flung toward walls
to regain
a delicate footing

work life
is one thing
we are told to believe is two
to be balanced
two sets of rules and priorities
two centers of gravity
two lives that must exist apart
one rotating earth under
one dancer
in you

It is almost time

Your hands
are poised on keyboard
to capture staff meeting takeaways

later pulling cash to pay for late night
slice and coffee
sinuous fingers pushing
ends of doughy crust
giving with a crunch
into a perfect fold
the steaming paper cup
balanced from bottom edge
on fingertips
They still work
years after
all of the notes
and ovations
An artist in an earlier age
Your detour now the route

You could transform
the graveyard of your dreams
or home-tap a budget
because you could be assistant to the chair one day
doors could open

It is almost time
when you place
what you can never forget
are still
the most musical hands of all
on that knob
and turn

me

You Won't Believe What I Did

i click
The Payoff is never as good as the tease
The Infinite Promise of the unknown
evaporates into obvious

i consider myself unnecessarily ordinary
pressing buttons to make the world
WONDROUS
inside
just to save something to my mind
i can offer
that makes you

click on me

squint
and lean back to take me in
because i seem brighter and bigger
than i was
when all i had was
me

113

This is idyllic
a Saturday morning slumber
Idle thoughts cohere into ideas
too anomalous
to note here

I mute my cell phone and pull out a book
of Anaïs Nin fever dreams
from the era she flouted fidelity
and gender rules

At the time it must have seemed so
risky
to live
consistent with her nature
in opposition to every useless law
and then to commit crimes
to paper
with indelible ink

Her restlessness
is my lucid dream
a time capsule held in hands
freshly perfumed with illicit embraces
a manual for me
to do almost anything
that is right
and set down
what I do
in lines that will float inside a warehouse of servers
a virtual confession booth of keywords

Inspired authenticity is an argument for innocence
or culpability for naiveté
words led Nin to life
Jesus to death
and me to this period.

A Single Decision Could Have Saved Me

There are quick journeys to dreams
entered with relief
and calm with closure
but other nights in which
manic manifestations of the day's jaws
need be muzzled for fear
nips invade sleep
pull the sheets down on my rest
tug at the mattress of me
churning the blood until they slap and
spill me yet again
unsustainably awake
I hear rain descending in sheets
from a nightmare that won't let go
no
here in the apartment
light walk follow sound bathroom
water covers the floor and rising
hot almost scalding
like it was boiling up from hell
the door pulled back
a waterfall of steam and liquid outside the pipe
I grab every towel in the closet and throw them down
wring a towel in the tub
hands already red from heat
and another
maybe a neighbor left the hot water running?
grab wring throw
grab wring throw
was I losing?
molten force crushing against hot water taps in
every apartment? grab wring throw
run run run upstairs door open spigot cracked her ceiling
when it blew
losing the battle while I'm there
and in that moment
hands already aching from effort
when a single decision could have saved me
from returning to the flood
and everything could have been washed away
so I could start anew with untroubled sleep

I ran

115

$7.25/hr Suite for Solo Voice

1. Prelude
What now?
don't know
I think
I need
to act

2. Allemande
This is not too hard
people here are nice
I like when it is busy
5AM's too early
for being made to dance

3. Courante
I hate not sleeping I
hate having to run to
bus running to work all
shift but it is cash

4. Sarabande
I think she likes me we
hooked up but my place lacks
She's worth a second job

5. Minuet 1/II
She definitely is worth it
But I am never home
She says that's why it's over
but this other girl
no

6. Gigue
I need to act
I cannot think
This is all there is
Dancing
The days
Away

They won't accept the obvious
Instead they march against us
Flaunting their disregard at the dangers they face
A many-headed beast whose limbs creep the nation
brainwashing children to embrace injustice
They want to have the conversation
But they won't listen
and there is nothing they can say
No alternative to us
to our absolute belief
to knowing and truth

It gets dark earlier every day
Some people must die
They will never stop protesting
Because we can never allow them the win
and there is no one willing
to order them to
stand down

This standoff is older
than us
than our nation
than existence
we carry the flag
so our descendants
will have something to think about and
a cause worth
handing down

Tomorrow will still be here
tomorrow
and won't be nearly as good
as it should
So feel good now

Say yes to revolution
They're not right with them
and fear the too too much chaos
at their scalding core

Expend all effort
on behalf of them
against them
on the pleasures of peace
that will come from
cradling every one of their faces
in sacred baptisms
outlasting breath

They lie:
There is no us
us is a rounding error
a cowardly retreat from freedom
to believe even one thing they don't
Everyone is them
Even you

Except for the other
them
the one doing crucifixions to too too many
They are the other other them

Blood is unburned ash

in the howl of blood-brushed lungs
my inside is screamed
tinged by heat
snaking smoke stinging away a life

here is my match
made of blood-filled arteries and veins
and ending at an explosive brain
with dendrite fuses that took forever to light
but are impossible to extinguish

I wanted to treasure you and sway
to music about hope under sunshine trees
swimming forever across a cool clean sky
to splash in air
shake up the salty sea inside
and make of us a love story

I am unmade
the unreality of hate
that we sacrificed so much
to keep alive
will need to be broken inside me
before I can unexplode
I will howl
at the fracture of a healing touch
every nerve resurrected
and then I will feel the unendurable anguish of our
rush to be our undoing
and dread
I am the only one defused
and everyone will be ashen sky

The Real You

In a slightly different order
the events of your life
would make you
a stranger
a seemingly scrambled confusion
an almost you
with an inconceivably ardent desire
to scratch out and chip away
every facet of
the real you
this almost you deeply grateful
your life would eventually be made
authentic
and how
looking back
it was
inevitable

Dysmorphia

This fight is indigestible
It roils and no
It is coming up inside me

We hurl rage at the defensive
so they become raw
like us
and ashamed at the shame they inflict
with their rage

We are
resolved
to forever defend against
their anger
eternally righteous
and ready to
lash out

And to pray for the night
our rage starts to boil in our guts
but not burn
instead prove palliative
a cement to make interior walls
into impenetrable fortress
so we can fight
even after we win

The sun makes borders out of skin
presses steel thumbs on skulls
and bellows radiation against our unhideable hides
our insides leaking out

Hard sodium lights pound our shoulders
until we collapse onto concrete
pinned amidst the tires and auto undersides
in shrinking space
smelling fumes
and pleading for softness

Screens stab needles of light
interrogation spotlights puncturing eyeballs
tattooing imprints of impediments
onto the sclera
ghosting inside us every time we blink

We are only whole in a dark
that's invisible
beyond outstretched fingers
in all directions
only there can we imagine
every bit of goodness possible
that begins with us
and expands
outward
forever

We make new memories
even in the act of remembering
To summon is to create
each anniversary a pulling down of towers and planes
endlessly first
a new bearing witness
as they sink ever more softly
behind a morning fog
of what once had been a clear blue sky
now so opaque it seems inevitable
this is the year
rows of obeli are supplanted
by those with fatal wounds
more freshly wrought
New children grieve upon this day
for the recently deceased
by sickness or blows at skin and through it into flesh
misperceptions forged into final curse
all red inside and too soon dead

Next year as the calendar strikes 11
family voices will rise and fall with each old loss resurrected
for them alone to suffer
44 names fading in the air
over unremarkable field
of strangers whose
hearts were stopped there
in unison
189 names fading in the air
of family members shut inside a 5-sided tomb
whose final thoughts were of anything
but the end
2,763 names fading in the air
where there had been breathing bodies in glass

Their loss shall be noted
until such time as we decree
that fog cover the ground
and these buildings and planes be left undisturbed
the families long forgotten
like descendants of Gettysburg
and new ones in their place
to claim the day

and mourn
their own
alone.

What inspires a person
to sign up for the wrong side
to swear on a life
to fight so
the right side
can't rebuild?

It might take some convincing
the enemy would think
or money or other perk
for us northerners to impose our way of life on an
independent nation of Confederates
or for us southerners to flout a moral imperative
to treat others like people
even slaves and Federalists

But it doesn't take much coaxing to sign-up for battles
powerful men are profligate barkers
exhorting defenders to think
like authors of bad war stories
whose every justification is proclaimed self-evident
our side proud, courageous and selfless
their side disposable agents of undifferentiated evil
socialists, nationalists, terrorists, zombies or imperial fighters

And yet we hold these truths to be self-evident:
are all born the same
may loudly strive for opportunities, joy and freedom
and live for love, friendship and peace
Only when desiring to deny others these rightful
dignities
do enemies commence to exist

We are only empty vassals
to the wrong side
patriotic vessels
to the right
when in truth everyone is alike
and in no way more important than this:

It is only each of us
who make enemies
of some of us

You!
Behold
Pollution
Smashed rubble of great cities
And architects' grand plans
Witness the pouring of freshly mixed cement
on new-leveled sites
and so much glass, a sign of trust that soon these mighty towers
this time
will stand

There will be parks and plazas
And the army stationed everywhere
to defend them to the death
Because it is the edict
that grand places and the chosen people are this eternal nation
And all will be for naught
if there be no one for you to yearn
to deeply, endlessly, shamelessly, unrestrainedly, desperately and loudly
love
or fear
only then shall their love make of this land, your home

Driven inside your mind
Reinforced inside your mind
Steel-plated and screwed inside you
You!

just like a prom
dress up and pose for pictures
give the camera a real stare down
you are not a child anymore
the shoes don't quite fit but you look great
your ride is here and it's getting late
final check you are nervous
but everyone is before heading out
I am so proud of you look how you've grown
this is your night

and then you wave goodbye and get into the car and
lucky you
you will martyr yourself for the cause
and blow up a hotel

We used to be free citizens
of all the land inside the USA
We have learned to be primal refugees and
monsters now more like you than they could ever be
You promised to die for us
We promise to live for you
We will kill them until they let us win
just to make us stop

politics danced with us
arms out and rigid
hands cocked
in the style of rote military follow-the-directions
misread demo drawing
peacock legs raised at backwards knee
and slammed down slide raise
a walz
of weak execution and strong needs
making potholes on dance floor

plastic plates, shovels and buckets
overfilled and oozing
with promises slathered in chloramine and turning meat
to keep us
waiting in a line
that writhes and slithers like a slug
dripping across the baking sidewalk
meals for bigger prey

The oration of stupid
is excreted
from low orifice
partially liquified
tie askew clanging
against decorum and expectation
to perfect effect
a perfect affect
of faux real
or real faux
the authentic posturing an exclamation point
that makes stupid
just like us
as we banter about the tie
and what it means
or how graceful he looks
when we glide across the floor
in his arms
and us in love forever

Offerings are selflessly
heroically
nightly
ritualistically made
to surviving nurses and
grocery store clerks
by us

(Half)
After any succumb
condolences are presented
like a folded flag

to the widower
the mother
and the son
by others

(Half)
whose losses are hidden under masks
solemn and reserved according to ancient norms
wailing and tears reserved
for the families of the fallen

(Fold Edge Upward into Triangle)
their fragile crashing and broken expressions
skinless like final decades had been
ripped
away and disappeared
and there was nothing to reach for
save this flag
on
the
way
down

(Repeat Until One Triangle Filled With Stars)
The flyover
The banging pots and pans
The eternally forgotten
Celebrated only when Stepping Up
and going to work while we stay safe
Loved And Admired genuinely

until This War Is Over
or they get sick and disappear
or we no longer feel
scared

(Fold Edge into Triangle)
and the rest of us move on
secretly relieved
there were enough Heroes in the world
so we did not need
to sacrifice
or later

(Present The Flag)
to have to remember

True story
a small child is on the road
in his only t-shirt and shorts
barefoot
cold
the sun blocked by one of many clouds passing through
unaware his father had told his neighbor
bring your son
then hurled his machete through shoulders
that boy about the same age then as
this boy's age now
unaware his clothes had been that same innocent child's
His father always regretting
not asking for shoes

The streets here don't have names but
each 3 by 3 meter section of land has a 3 word address
that the boy mutters as he walks
Home has always been measured squares of space
one pretty much like another
except only some have arms

True story
You will now turn the page

131

We rape, cheat, enslave and murder each other

Infect and addict ourselves
feed fine particulates to lungs
and pocket the change
We know this is not right
We know this is not normal behavior

Then we make movies and articles about
suffering
as idle diversions from our days
to watch and proclaim ourselves ahead

So be entertained and
aware of what's trending
Say you are woke
or never would be
Proclaim how wrong it is
what they do
to themselves
and how lucky you
are you
know good people

Huddle behind locks
as you sing lullabies
it isn't your responsibility you are not we
you gave this you told that you you you you you
you make up lies
so you can sleep
But no one deserves release from our burden

We rape, cheat, enslave and murder each other
We are normalizing
the unacceptable
and thus become normal
Normal is what we agree to accept

You
so tiny
will be sunk

On the long march from there to there
across the in-between
each muddy footstep a reminder of rock

on this place
a girl and boy met
where the temple that would unite them
was built
even before the first home
from wood in
forgotten forest
you are a distant branch
on their family tree
and three billion years ago
two animals
so tiny
battled to the death
to win the right to mate
and you
descended from the winner
on that very spot
and a forest grew
the ground settled and squeezed and
aged and was made rock a hundred feet down
bubbling up as pebbles
one entering your shoe
at this very spot
that you can't shake out
until you don't even feel it
and it becomes a part of you
a forgotten souvenir
at the middle
of the journey
of all of us.
At every step.

My Hands Are Better Than My Body

First I carried disease on my hands like a surface gangrene
repulsed and desperate to make them safe before
I touched face and was invaded
by an enemy poised to use my blood to breed

Then I carried the pandemic lightly

And finally
I imagined
not at all

After months of disinfection under faucets
bending and unbending fingers
legato interlocking and sliding
swirling one hand around the ball of the other
with silky soap and
warm water
suds risen and rinsed
my skin is cleansed
and perfect and safe
I am frequently restored
yet changed
for each moment a nerve had fired while rubbing
it marked the occasion
and a conspiracy of sensation
has emerged
emergency sensors
beneath palms, fingers, wrists and backs
set so sensitive as to
drown out the rest of me
in a sensuous bath

now hands
are a delicious reminder of how good it can feel
to remain alive

CSAR

Insights and granted wishes are like jewels
I drop into your vast unlit crevasse
I wait for the "ting" of one striking a side
or bottom
or a flash from polished facet
catching light from above
revealing a path up and out
but there is only darkness
and no sound save the ringing in ears
from whoops of triumph and shouts of
exultation
as we stood atop the chest of treasure
hard won through digging
We claimed it for ourselves, remember?
each shiny object a proclamation
that rewards follow commitment
a promise of answers
in every retrieved stone

You're lost with no way up
and I cannot go back
so I offer you everything we ever wanted
and that helped us escape
rubies, diamonds and gold
all I have
in the hope you consider them worthy of feet
and you can climb

At last there is one man
who was a stranger schooled and loved and loving
seasoned and preparing outside of your awareness

No promise of joy is unmitigated
this stranger was a miracle
who could not matter
until after others loved you
with half-frowns
and interminable incompletion

Your first meeting so fertile with hope
now harvested
Relief and love
the fruits so long sought
infuse your wedding day
with sweetness
You got the ring
and everything he would offer
was all you ever wanted:
a public promise
a key never to be returned
a husband to share your home
to adore you
cherish you
a hand to forever hold yours
and that your hearts be internally and indelibly inscribed:
everything meant less
until that moment
someone meant everything

Pieces of a Whole

was it your beautiful face
and teasing hint of perfection beneath dress
or the effort
you might have made
to make it look
effortless?

was the achingly easy grace in your smile
rehearsed in mirrors
honed in previous performances
or made by parents
and handed down
one more thing from toes to hair
carelessly or carefully rendered?

either you have manufactured yourself
like a student made into virtuoso
whose faculties
move people
to longing for
well composed pieces of a whole
or you were born this way
a natural whose gifts lay not in creating
but in giving in
resigned to reject any greater promise
more remote

You tell me
everyone has a beautiful smile
and knows how to inspire smiles
in others
that today matters
and you are living
with feeling
and I am thus unmade
and then
remade
into me

Dye does not change the color of hair
it is a disguise which hides the gifts of time and ancestors
to deny heritage and proclaim myself
better
than the history of me
whether squandered or a curse
a me to be manufactured
out

what is ambition but a dissatisfaction?
a crossing of the line from acceptance to desire
re-imagining the timeline
while I prove fit
to speed backwards toward dreams
of when I was possible
authenticity restored
only by a willingness to change back

I cannot know whether
these ornaments beautify the tree
or make it look
artificial
I will trim old branches
treat autumn as second spring
unshackled to age or inheritance
for now
a man with an unlimited future

in that part of town
the painters of faces
will be in self-portrait party poses
more aspirational at their fade
than ever at first easy hungers
modeling the behavior of living
as art installation
accumulating data on the location
dopamine levels and electrical activity
the adrenaline increase from finger on doorbell
the light level inside the home, facial recognition
judgment of clothing and subsequent self-re-evaluation
to make the work compelling

then there will be smiles:
genuine evolutionary artifacts and
joy
and their art will be lost
for awhile
suddenly unimportant
thought less authentic than a hug
grateful relief
living
though loving life is the epitome of what their art aspires to inspire

creating a more impactful work can involve observation
at slight remove to
know context and how life resonates within others
an analysis of how
love looks from the other side of the door
before the finger touches bell

Art and poetry and clothes and manners and words
are heartfelt facsimiles of feelings
subject to norms and rules
occasionally broken
to make a work more real
each is an artist's byproduct of love or longing
imperfect and idealized offerings
to those not yet fully convinced
or to art lovers
lovers
in celebration of art

of the person who created it
or yet another attempt
to change or preserve the world

I remove my clothes and don
a paper gown
the blinds open facing the sidewalk
and the light is on
I sit on the exam table and look anywhere but the window
wordless in an empty room
and consider whether I am hot or cold
and nervous after so many appointments
I look for air vents
should they heat the space a few extra degrees
for the unclothed?
but how should I hi no
I'm comfortable, thanks fine nothing I've noticed
blood quick exam vitals thanks you can dress
brief and friendly and comforting
each efficient inquiry inviting perfunctory response
fluids will tell the story of me

Someday perhaps, I will ponder my decisions on everything
after my actions become meals that trigger chemical responses
menus one day making unhelpful meat
I will wonder whether there was
a question I should have asked
before it was too late

the blinds open facing the sidewalk
and the light is on
I sit on the exam table and
look anywhere but the window

you must often forget how special it is to be you
and how others imagine what it's like
to move through each grand adventure

instead you navigate small moments
like walking through kitchen
not noting the achievements
that led to the rightness of each fixture
focussed instead on the retrieval of glasses, liquids and ice
and the distracting minutia of schedule conflicts
and deadlines
or the next wondrous thing you are
aiming to do
like all of us
looking with anticipation toward
the best moments of life you are sure lie ahead
if only this one thing goes right
that "one thing" forever supplanted
if reached at all
so a quiet dread is never allowed
to sprout
that the ascent is over
and each day is a bloodletting
of your gifts

even in unquiet moments
a better life lies
in rejecting escapes into lives of others
such as Nicodemus of John
a bit player in a big story
whose throne was desired by a sculptor not fully made
his anguish causing chisel to
misfire and destroy his own tomb
the Nicodemus of Michelangelo
clothed in the artist's face
whose ancient wings enclosed and held up
Jesus, Mary and the church
his true audacity arriving too late
for mortal hands to make right
living his dying days proclaiming in stone
that he could assume the mantle of another
all
for nothing

BreatheEasy Walden Apartments is located on the former site of
Walden Pond once considered nature, a lingering threat to humans and
all things manufactured from thought.
Nature runs the program which cc's viruses, dirt invaders and other
predators in order to destroy
humanity and its great works.
Walden Pond was saved by a book
universally considered boring and unreadable.
It spawned a small fanatical Environmentalist Cult bent on
the surrender and subjugation of humanity.
On their defeat the book's last remaining copy was ceremoniously
deleted at what is now
the BreatheEasy Walden Apartments site
along with the trees, pond, the author's cc'd hovel and playground.
Playgrounds were for stupids and undesirables during
The DUH Age
as were bothersome reading standards
before our JOYOUS RETURN TO EDEN.
BreatheEasy Walden Apartments is abundant in
screens, games, videos, apps, politics,
engaging conspiracies, drugs, alcohol, porn, cooling stations,
militias for hire, affordable oxygen

I focus on driving
the days are now mile markers on a one way road
in the almost relenting heat of late summer
[mile]
across land seemingly familiar but haunted
with light like old movie night scenes
daylight shot then
dimmed so slightly we scarcely notice
moving forward on a single tank

the sun makes its lazy way across the sky
[mile]
lighting others walking and driving in
lanes close enough to see
I wave
we're on this journey together
[mile]
comparing summer notes
through open windows and rarely
stories about winter lands
unimaginable
[mile]
where the season has advanced
to permanent night
the very atmosphere giving way to an occlusion
and what warm air remains
is wedged
up and away until the end of time
and all molecular motion
stops

still the sun moves and it's already fall and the leaves
are turning and I pull a sweater from the back seat
[mile]
remove my sunglasses
take a look at the landscape in case
I might be missing something then
focus on driving

144

There are no degrees of life
It is rigorously binary
even when lost and brought back
No dimmer switch
to raise on awakening
or lower at sleepy
it's even considered at full when the heart beats
but the brain has gone silent

From nothing we come to life.
no break eyes open
and who would ever want to lose any of this?
we are exhausted at the pace
but the switch is on
and what's next what's next what's next
sleep and what's next
we are unrelenting

Yet every moment of life is filled with gradation
with subtlety and contradiction
ifs buts thoughs and other
words our progenitors made
to manage changes in perception
misperceptions
shifting and competing priorities
We choose to manage it better
by ignoring it all
living in the absolute
rigorously binary
we are always right
our beliefs are us
shed not when proven false
but only at the point
they hurt too much
Thus do we make myths of
ourselves as we float
towards the off switch
and coax others
to agree with us
on everything

Lean

when born we lean
and learn too late
there never was a wall
just air
giving way and nestling
in our slipstream
idle banter
seeming to rise
like chimney smoke heating sky
but it's just our mouth
descending
as we move closer to
stopping
It is impossible to imagine
for we only know
how to fall

it is not supposed to be this way
we have faith we will
stand
pray to it
give alms do acts of kindness and penance

then the hardest knock
that no one feels
a sideways slap
into dreamless always
and we will be abandoned by the very air
that followed us down
We should see our path
but all we do
is stare back at where we've been
and believe it will last

146

Will you choose to be sunk early in dirt
because you think
there is somewhere else to go?
No.
But you might believe death brings a reward
worth more than tomorrow's sunrise

You can live with death
forever shed the vanishing Now
that is the only time you have known
though it is in the covenant
you signed up for
that you must give up family
No more feeling their flesh beneath fingers
Goodbye to the warm glow of Thanksgiving

Maybe you're right and there will be
an even better place for you
after life
and the same kind of otherworldly technology that made you so good
will make you
exactly as intended after your transfer to after
I hope so
whoever wired earth and got it going
so smoothly and well and
kind
must have tweaked some switches and turned some knobs
where you are heading
to give you something to look forward to now:
a happy ever after place to fill your thoughts
while your body empties of all but bone

147

Latency

"I am
Supposed to be
Responsible
To those
who
Depend
on
Me."

Those skinny words save lives
and make a famine of us
invaluable and restorative as last alternative
yet not worthy of a pauper's purse
hammered into our pliable dented skulls
until we bleed out disbelief
and succumb to dull throbbing duty
obligated only to this scarring sacrilege hailed as saintly

My mother told me what we should do
and about what she did herself until she was gone
She did it all for love

String

A Partridge amongst pears thinks it is a story about string.
String keeps the Partridge stuck in a tree alone.
Somewhere, two Turtle Doves and three French Hens are tied together
by string.
Somewhere three French Hens and two Turtle Doves are tied together
by string.
String keeps the Partridge stuck in a tree alone.
A Partridge amongst pears thinks it is a story about string.

Miracles

The finger

The touch

The seismic shake

The whisper

The speaking bodies

In unison

Now singing to love

The morning which follows

The unpacking

Unions and reunions

The births

The last goodbye

The whisper

The finger

The touch

Miracles

There was so much to say
like what mattered
and how to make things right
Her hands rested softly on the lectern
The mic too high but she tilted her head
trying to be heard above the cocktail hour
din
and dinner band's
sound check of
"Live and Let Die"

Then there was nothing left to say
so she turned
and took a single step
the spotlights and some eyes glaring at her
and another step
is it habit or a need to please
that causes the head to turn and hand to rise?
and another step
the hand to wave?
and another
and the smile
from what depth did it rise?
and another
was she mourning underneath a mask or was this
who she really was ?
and another
and another
and another
darkness

and another

In-Between

Silence

is the room

between walls

not the walls where art hangs

nor the speakers emitting piles

of pleasure

to make us

full

it is the space

we empty

after

and fill

with

Silence

A seagull in the sky
circles overhead with eyes beaded on flashes
of silver in the depths
then arcs into a heavy dive
as if violently sucked
from air by ocean

Below me two creatures meet
a fish intimately pierced
by an inconceivable invader
from an impossible place

waves are like flip card horse gallops
an ever-repeating ocean of troughs
each a stutter of air between salt water summits
the space where some creatures breathe
and others choke

Today is a Saturday of other's plans

the gull emerges with a quivering fish in its beak
a normal day in every way
this is my time
above and under cresting waves
to float
timeless
silently
breathing

This is the full measure of a breath
that was a moment before
inert atmosphere
an insignificant
part of the onion skin shell of earth
in constant motion and mixing
since the firmament cohered

my lungs fill
with a few molecules breathed by Mohandas Gandhi
James Baldwin
the first dinosaur and you
inside me, too, as you read this and breathe in
a few molecules I'd once held
perhaps as I was writing these lines
to maintain the momentum of this life

yes, admittedly just a few particles
not enough to matter
this poem similarly small
but if you look deep enough inside
you will find me
all the people you know
and pieces of you that will become
pieces of everyone who will ever live until the very last
breath

Imagine

If you would stop what you're doing
To listen
Think
Really
Really think
How much more is
possible

Inevitable

if only
You listen
Stop
Think
Really
Really think
How much is
possible

Four Hands in Morning

Our hands rise from the covers like intertwining suns
a corona of dancing fingers
over sliding palms and knuckles
forming a single silhouette against the ceiling
soaked in grey-blue pre-dawn sky
lodestars united
our true north
orienting us into our future

Brows lower
at the touch that bends the hands
sunsets arms
unlocks the fingers
to find our faces
and pull us
into a
kiss

Inevitably
enroute
hands will be emptied of hands
and two hands will rise in mourning
loss has no inherent value
so we create it
as we created north
to find our way

We all need something to last forever
these are the last cherished words I will share

they won't change anything
any more than a last pebble dropped in the middle of a pond
it is noteworthy only in that there is nothing to follow it
down
the concentric circle expanding and undisturbed by further turbulence
this final touch
a kiss of stone and still water
done
the center mark on surface once again smooth
the sepulchral stone resting on the bottom
silt descended onto it
a funereal veil of lace

this short stanza was composed long ago
revisited and left as you are reading it now
the work complete
even as the circle from stone continues outward
like an echo of an ending
the shudder that follows the realization
your body reacting
a ripple
after it's gone
glass

Breathe.

light color. sound? stumble fall hands palm flat stumble stumble turn
light swirls.
light color. person movement good? movement repeat. good.
movement repeat. good. good. good.

click-click……….. tap-tap-tap-tap-right-tap-tap-right-right…..jump
…….click-tap….tap…..left-tap-tap…..tap-tap-tap-tap-jump-right-left
tap-tap-right-tap-tap-tap-tap-tap- jump…music….colors….light………

Sneakers on hard soil, a lane in thick woods, young saplings striving on
rocky, leaf-strewn slope, indifferent to the old trees they will one day
become. Final turn in shadow then
sun, treetops a floor, no higher to go.
Stop.

Turn page. Turn page. Turn page. Oh. Turn page. Huh. Turn page. I
think I understand now. Turn page. Turn page I had no idea. I might
want to share this. Turn page. Turn page. Turn page. Turn page.
Turn page. Freeze. Blink. Cry. Wisdom.

Soft lips. Hands on shoulders back yearning urgent hopeful hands
asking permission. Soft lips. Body relaxes or stiffens.
Zipper.

Music. Step. Step. Step. Step. Step. Step. Step. Step. Step. Step. Step.
Step. Step. Step. Step. Step. Step. Turn. Turn. Turn. Speak. Hand
forward. Receive a ring. Hand down. Take a ring. Insert ring on fourth
finger. Lower hands. Move in. Embrace. Kiss. Step.

A baby. (light color. sound?)

A job well done. (no higher to go. Stop.)

Breathe. Breathe. Breathe. Breathe. Breathe. Breathe. Breathe. Breathe.
Breathe. Breathe. Breathe. Breathe. Breathe. Breathe. Breathe. Nod.
Smile. Comfort. Hold hands. Breathe. Wave. Breathe. Close eyes.
Breathe. Breathe. Breathe. A job well done.

Breathe.

Acknowledgments

I am grateful to:

Taryn Herbert and Larry Young, artists who were flint to my rock on that auspicious night, their spark lighting my night. This book is here only because they were there.

Early readers: Holly, Gordon, Holly, Taryn, Larry, Michael and Aldara.

Later readers: Holly, Kate, Heather, Karen, Shane, Roy, Rose, Zoe and Annette

Audrey Frischman and The Public Theater for ensuring "Watch Me Work" worked well, and especially the profoundly generous and insightful Suzan-Lori Parks for wisdom, inspiration, energy and writing time, in twenty-minute chunks, that I spent on quite a number of works in these pages. This book would have been shorter and shallower without her.

Those who inspired a work or two (or more) whose modesty and discretion requires they be unnamed here. Simply know they are each beautiful and worthy of more than any clumsy prose I could compose here.

Most of all to my family, each of whom carpe diem. Thank you for your love, your joy and your greatness.

CPSIA information can be obtained
at www.ICGtesting.com
Printed in the USA
LVHW011558151022
730779LV00003B/359